Dreamers Are Achievers!

DREAMERS ARE ACHIEVERS!

Classes 806, 807, 808, 809 and 810
Virgil I. Grissom, JHS 226

This book belongs to: ______________________

Step/Write Into Your Greatness
was commissioned by
Rushell S. White, Principal
Virgil I. Grissom, JHS 226
New York City Department of Education

A Poetic Motivations, LLC Publication

Renée McRae, President
Poetic Motivations, LLC
www.poeticmotivations.com

Dreamers Are Achievers!

A Compilation of Poetry by Students of
Classes 806, 807, 808, 809 and 810

Virgil I. Grissom, M.S. 226
121-10 Rockaway Boulevard
Ozone Park, NY 11420

Principal
Rushell S. White

Assistant Principals
Juliet Adams
Michele Cohen
David Possner
James Randall
Jennifer Shirley-Brown

Participating Teachers
Mr. Zeigler
Mr. March
Ms. Sanghavi

Renée McRae
Poet-in-Residence

Introduction

These eighth graders were the best! Each class was amazing, and I enjoyed every moment of working with them individually and collectively in their *'DREAMERS ARE ACHIEVERS!'* anthology. These students wrote ballads, raps and limericks about different topics, including their aspirations, hopes, fears, beliefs and dreams!

Thank you to MS 226 Virgil I. Grissom's Principal, Ms. Rushell White. Her belief in the "Step/Write Into Your Greatness" workshop program is evidenced by the opportunity she has granted us to work with her students. Thank you to my participating teachers, Mr. March, Mr. Zeigler and Ms. Sanghavi, who were so gracious and helpful in sharing their students with me and writing poetry alongside them..

Big shout out and thanks to Ms. Shirley for coordinating the program and being there for every question (and favor) along the way; and of course, Ms. Posy, for always helping out with paperwork (even in the midst of her own busy teaching schedule).

A special thank you goes out to Mr. Tariq McKay, School Counseling Manager, Queens South Borough Field Support Center, for the initial recommendation to Virgil I. Grissom, MS 226. Special acknowledgments to our production team for tirelessly typing and proofreading, Jacqueline Collins and Christa Victoria.

Special thanks to Mr. Daniel Carlton, poet, actor, producer, who worked with the students on writing a piece to the quote "It's not what you look at, it's what you see."

To Classes 802, 804, 805, 806, 809 and 810:

Remember this: "There are no Benches on the Road to Success."
Lucy Marie Burns

Much Love, & Many Blessings to You!

Renée McRae
a/k/a Ms. Renée

When I think of friendship
I think of you the most
Because you are always there for me
You're the butter on my toast
The French to my fries
The tissue to my cries

When I think of friendship
You're the one I call
Your name is on my tongue
Because you never let me fall

Always got my back
Keeping me on track
Got my secrets in your heart
We've been loyal from the start

When I think of friendship
I'm glad that I have you
Because if you were not in my life
I wouldn't have a clue

Renée McRae

(Dedicated to Mr. McRae)

Friendships

FEARS

CAREERS

DREAMS

Confidence

TALENTS

Dreamers Are Achievers!

Special Thank You!

Ms. White
Principal

Ms. Shirley
Asst. Principal
(Coordinator)

Mr. Zeigler
807, 808, 809

When I am successful
Wait, who says I ain't there now?
Some define success as the amount of money
you amass
To those I'd tell to kiss my
Assume you were filthy broke
Like not having a dime to your name
But were wealthy with a great family
Could success be the blame?
See, success means many things
To a host of people
To some it's the collection of material things
To others it's how much of the world you see
flying upon wings
To me success is what I want it to be
A wife, some kids, maybe a lil' doggie
Maybe my success will be defined by position
In my career, my drive, my determination
My lack of fear

MR. ZEIGLER

Friends
How many of us have them?
Best friends, the til-the-end friends
The 'make you forget about what's bothering
you' type friends, those are the best kind
I promise you

The kind to have your back
To go with you to Hell and back
The 'lift you off the floor
When you hurting' type

What about them other ones
The ones that are always never there
You know them bums
The ones you always invite
But they never show up to support you
You know them type
The ones you tell your all to
And they just give you confusion
To go through

The ones that stab you in the back
From the front

Them the worst type
They swear they tough
But wouldn't bust a grape
In a fruit fight

How 'bout those that always keep
You on your toes
The ones that keep it real
Regardless of how real, real gets

The 'stand by your side'
(When you outside)
Won't misguide
Your life—They help revise
Make your day better
To no surprise
Be there through your best and
Love you through your worst
Them the friends
I call friends
Them forever
They come first

MR. ZEIGLER

If I Could

If I could make a choice to float or sink
Honestly, sinking may be better
Than floating

Sinking, you reach depths
Where there are no distractions
No boundaries—Just limitless peace
Depth has its mystery and
Floating comes with too many problems

Imagine floating and those that can't float
Just eager to hate your growth
Growing up is hard
It has its down sides

You have to deal with
Pain, struggle, anger, obstacles
On the road to success

Now don't believe any of the aforementioned
I could never settle for failure
I'd rather deal with the rough journey
To appreciate flying high
And overcome all obstacles
I may face

See, failure is easy—just like death
Is guaranteed
So why waste what you can never get back?
Time is of the essence
Waste it or catch me at the top
If you could

MR. ZEIGLER

I Have the Power

I have the power to influence young minds
One brand new thought at a time
I can deposit gems that grow
Into priceless pieces of art years from now

Something small may seem worthless
At first
But what happens when you mold it,
Care for it, love it, share it
Can it grow?
What happens to a rainy day
When the sun comes out?
Does it clear up all the pain
And make things okay?
Or does it just mask confusion
Just to reapply it thicker
Like a double coat of paint?

Can you make better
What's already bad?
Of course, you can

Just add some sun
Care for it some
Love it more
And you, too, can create
Priceless contributions to
This place we call . . .
LIFE

MR. ZEIGLER

Mr. March
806, 809, 810

Mice run, down the hall
See them go
Chase a ball

Once it's summer
Now it's fall
See them go
Chase and all

Run mice run
Though you fall
DNA
Of Love will call

MR. MARCH

Ms. Sanghavi
810

You Think You Know Me

You think you know me
But you really don't see
What is really
Inside of me

You think you know me
But you really don't feel
The broken spirits
I can heal

You think you know me
But you really don't hear
The words of strength
I can steer

You think you know me . . .

MS. SANGHAVI

MR. MARCH
Class 806

Alisha Alexander
Asif Amiroola
Khameraj Amrit
Clint Bridgelal
Amir Dean
Brian Delgado
Kelly Delgado
Christopher Dookram
Isaiah Drepaul
Kailyn Gooden
Tashawn Howard
Eliana Hurtte
Kevon Indarsingh
Narima Khan
Keshan Latchman
Trinity Lewis
Jared Maitlall
Jaliya Norman
Anyely Nunez
Arianna Pascoe
Kasey Quick
Tennyson Raghubir
Hemdutt Ramlall
Munesh Ramoutar
Keelin Rodriguez
Recheal Rogers
Jahiel Stewart
Jahmar Sullivan
Darell Tavarez

Class 806

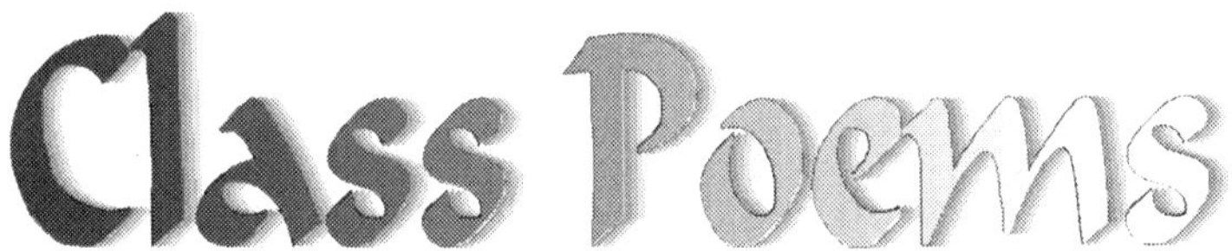

From Class 806

A Class Poem is a poem that happens from a brainstorming session. Different students call out lines and we collaborate until we are satisfied.

Respected by all because she is an
Energetic poet not attracted to
Negativity who helps her students
Evolve into positive role models with
Effective dreams and intellectual conversation

From Class 806

A Class Poem is a poem that happens from a brainstorming session. Different students call out lines and we collaborate until we are satisfied.

There once was a chicken bone
That was laying on the street alone
Along came a pup
And picked it right up
And then the puppy went home

WORD WALL
WORD WALL

Thankful!

I'm thankful for my mom because
She buys me things, takes care of me
And loves me unconditionally
My mom may yell at me
But she does what's best for me
We have our ups and downs
But we will never hate each other
I couldn't ask for another mom
Because she's the best mother

Alisha Alexander

You think you know me but you don't
You're gonna see me on 5th Avenue
Owning a Gucci store
Five or more
While you sit in front of my Gucci store
Begging for 15 cents
And eating donuts off the floor
And I'm still on top
No one can stop me now

When I was a little boy
About 9 years old
This man with glasses
Walking past my school every day
And staring at me
I always wondered how and what he was looking for
And why was he looking at me

Asif Amiroola

If I could eat food, I would
It's so tasty
If I could
I might even eat a pastry
If I could, I would fight for it
Ain't no way you're getting it
So don't even think about taking it

KHAMERAJ AMRIT

Dragon Ball Z is the greatest show of all time

Raging Blast 2 is a video game from the franchise

Action at its best

Gou is Vegeta's rival

Objects of wish-granting power are the dragon balls

Never going to end in my heart

Beerus is the god of destruction in DBZ

Amazing storylines

Last to none

Living in our world

Zenoverse

CLINT BRIDGELAL

When I grow up, no one will stop me
When I grow up, I will be set free
To grow like a tree
Everyone will see
Trust me and believe
You will wanna be me
Because in my future
I will be in a place
Where everyone can look at
My success to trace

Amir Dean

I'm thankful for my family
Because they are all friendly
I'm thankful for my phone
It gets me in a happy tone

I'm thankful for my shoes
They're something I will never lose
I'm thankful for my brother
I wouldn't want another

We all have this trust
That will never be lost
I'm thankful for the food we eat
I'm honest and I'll never cheat

I'm thankful for this poem
Which brings the heat

Spiderman is amazing because his

Palms shoot webs. He

Is determined to stop

Doc Oc because he is

Evil. His boss is J. Johan Jameson who is

Really strict and thinks that Spider

Man is a menace

Anyone who does not enjoy him is

Not cool

Brian Delgado

"It's not what you look at that matters; it's what you see"

The customer in the store
He was weird
And always entered the store at 6:30
He always had the brown hat on
And was very quiet
He always walked around my block
Twice
At 7:00 P.M.

Bully when he is playing

Runs when he gets the ball

Attacks the other team

Defensive against the other team

Yet he still makes the touchdown!

CHRISTOPHER DOOKRAM

The best of the best
Running beyond the limit
Acting like the rest
Could I give it my very best
Keeping up with the crew
So I can know what to do

ISAIAH DREPAUL

What I am thankful for is Jesus
When we need help, he never leaves us

When we are feeling sad or mad
He cheers us up and makes us glad

In the heat he makes us cool with air
He is also very fair

Some people think he is Black
Some say he is White
But all he does is shine his light

He created the sun and heat
And all the food we love to eat

KAILYN GOODEN

If I could go back in time
I would, no doubt
Even if we're arguing
I just want to hear your mouth

If I could scream out
Loud in the street, I would
Loud and angry
But only in the woods

No one would understand why
I like trees and bushes
The only reason why I feel this way
Is because no one is looking

Tashawn Howard

I'm thankful for food
Food is the yin to my yang
It fills me up
It helps me survive
Without food I'm nothing

Eliana Hurtte

"It doesn't matter what you look at ... it only matters what you see."

One day I saw a big house that was so dark

It had lights inside but no cars in the driveway

Then I saw a weird person with a hoodie on

I don't know if it was a person or not

but every minute I heard a squeaky sound like a rat

Furthermore, the person with the hoodie started looking at me

Then I started to run away so fast, like a cheetah

And I never came back the following day

Kevon Indarsingh

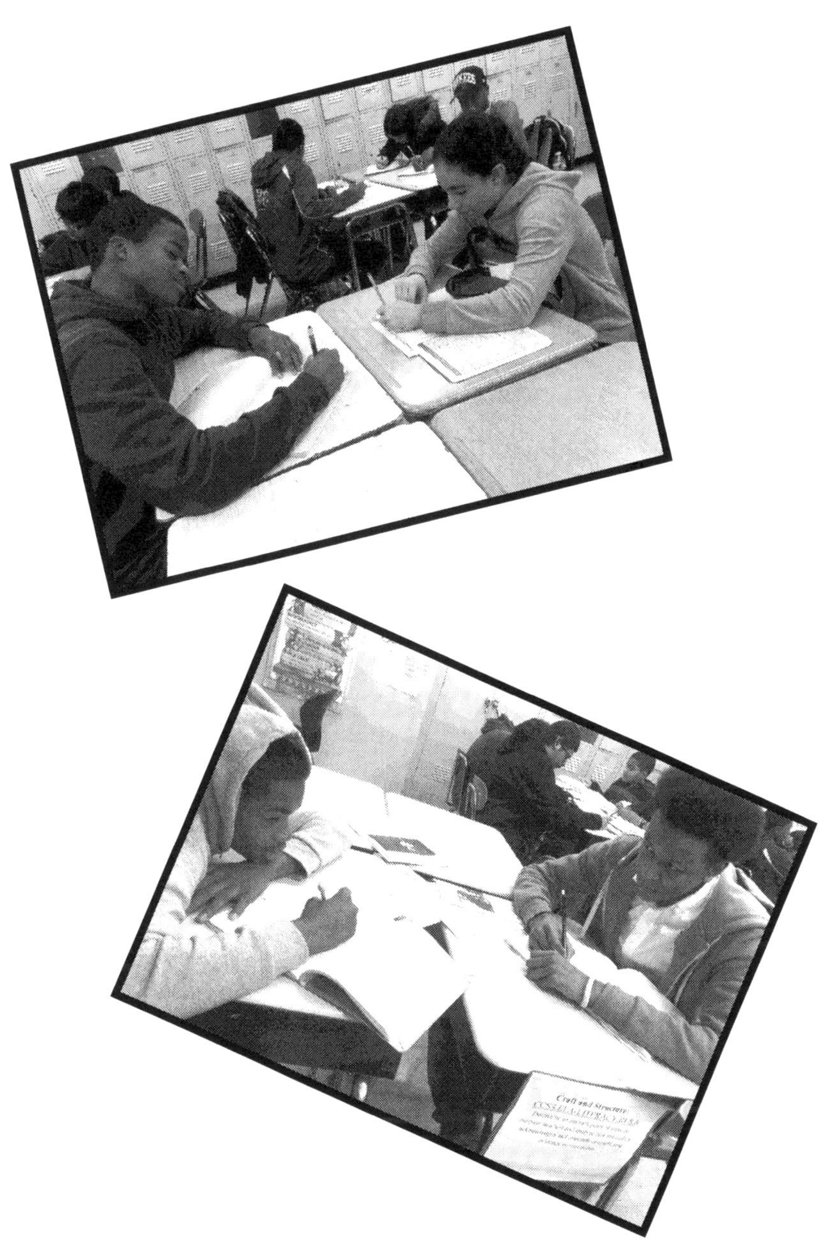
Craft and Structure

Through tears and fights
Through smiles, I knew everything
Would be alright

Through love and hate
Through betrayal and debate
For you, I'll always have faith

Being your best friend
I know this relationship will never end
By your side I will stand
And you'll stand by mine, too
Because that's what best friends do

NARIMA KHAN

All I ever needed was you
You said you needed me, too
But I don't think that's true

I listened to all you needed to say
During the hard times
I even said "I love you"
About a million times

I don't actually say that to anyone
But you were my best friend
That I don't think I could ever let go
I gave you all the love that you needed
But now you turned out to be a big fat lie

I always trusted you
Like you were part of my life
But now that part has died
Now you're here begging to be my friend
Because there's no one like me
But for me you're just nobody

When I first met you, I was stunned
Like someone shot me with a gun
I hoped we could be friends
Hopefully more than that
Damn, you were so fine
I fell right into your trap

We became friends
Then fell in love
Our relationship
So fine
It fit like a glove

We were in love
Until that day
You took a trip to Club Getaway
You texted me, saying everything went wrong
That text so long
I thought it was a song

A week later, I saw you and him
Holding hands
I was so nervous
I could have used a fan

Always see you guys in the hallways
Always ruining my day
Every time I see you
I try to look away

You said no one could ever replace me
Looks like he did that, now I see
I was living in past memories
I know now "us" was just a fantasy
I wasn't the right one, now I see
But don't come crying back to me

KESHAN LATCHMAN

Trinity is my name and I
Really am
Interested in fashion. I am
Not interested in drama
Interested also in art, it requires
Time and practice
You think I'm

Lying but I love shapes and patterns
Each shape and color is
Wonderful in its own way
I love fashion and art
See what I'm doing, I'm being creative

When I look into my future
I see myself
Looked up on a computer
Being a big star
Making enough money
To travel really far
I will look back
To when I was a little boy
And how as I grew up
Mother Nature was my toy
I will be a ball player
I will play so hard
Just like a ball slayer

Friendship is caring
It starts with a talk
Friendship would last longer
Than Jack in the Beanstalk
Friendship is special
Like a wish
It's like holding my breath
But not like a fish
All we do
Is chill and hang out
From that moment
Friendship starts to spout
Being a friend
Means a lot
A good friend
Is what I've got

JARED MAITALL

When I look into the future
I will forget about all of my sadness and hurt
I want to see lights and cameras
And all of my fans going berserk
My parents will be proud
My family will be proud
They will be chanting my name
So very loud
I won't care about the fame or money
I will care about how nobody shot me down

Jaliya Norman

If I could, I would turn back time
I miss you, I want you back
The world is so dark without you
If I could I would bring you back
I miss your hair, your smile and your voice
I don't understand why you had to go
I miss you, Grandma
I hope you are having a good time up there

If I could I would
Change the world to be a better place
Don't let the negativity take us away
No harm, no fear
Just be yourself and you will
See the new you appear
Although the road is rough
Just listen to your soul
Let it be your gear
And the new ideas will appear

Anyely Nunez

There is always a mystery in his eyes
That I would never define
He looks alone
With no one by his side
He lost hope in himself
But he is still alive
In his mind he'd rather
Let them eat him inside
Than speak about
What his life is really like

Mom, you pick me up when I fall
You wipe away my tears
When I rode my bike, you were there
My first fight, you released my rage into thin air
You make me noodles when I'm hungry
Although that was unnecessary to say
I love you, Mom, with all my heart
And that was very necessary to say
God forbid anything happen to you, I would decay
Into a miserable existence, I have to say
I will never stop loving you with all my heart
And even when you leave me for work in the morning
My love for you will never depart

Arianna Pascoe

I laugh at people who think they know me
Y'all don't know who I am or who I even wanna be
See, y'all don't know my past
Y'all don't know the "old me" really
It's the same me, I ain't never changed
I will always be the same
Watch me change the world
While you're watching me on tv
Wishing you could be me
See, I'm like the wind
You hear me but you can't see me
So, don't step up to me like you know me
Stay in your lane because I'm hitting the gas
And I'm not stopping
You can just watch me moving
Man, I'm gone

Kasey Quick

You think you know me to just stop and stare
And make me shake in fear
You think you know me, then think again
You wasted a thought. Oh man, not again
You think you know me, trying to spread the word
All you're doing is acting like a turd
You think you know me, I'm a friend to the end
But if you slip, I can turn and bend
And pop up like a popular trend

TENNYSON RAGHUBIR

Track is my life
You can't stop me
And if you can
I will run for my life
Track is so important to me
You won't understand

Friendship comes and goes
It's all about loyalty and faith
Friendship is a key to love
That you should cherish and
Keep in a safe place

HEMDUTT RAMLALL

Humor is one thing my friends and I share
Even though we make fun of each other, we still care
But still, we do our work and "oh yeah, she's a nerd."
And sometimes we even sing the bird is the word
Even though she is not here right now there is no doubt
What my friends and me are all about

MUNESH RAMOUTAR

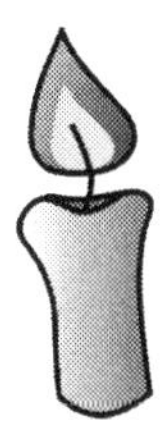

If I could, I would stop war
And fewer people would die
Then fewer people would cry
Pain and suffering might dim down
And all the evil would die
And that's what I would do
If I could

My soul, dim and dark
But somewhere I know
There's a spark
And with that spark
I know there's a flame
And that flame will shine so bright
And that flame will light my night

Keelin is awesome

Excited to have a great family

Especially loves her family

Loves her best friends, Kelly, Eliana, Jahiya, Alisha

Is smart

Never gives up

KEELIN RODRIGUEZ

Riding through the city
Eating a hotdog with chili on the side
It's so hot, it burns my eyes
Even though I want to eat it all
I ain't, 'cause I'm gonna lose control

Recheal Rogers

Jahiel is my name
And basketball is my game. I can make a
Half court shot
In basketball, 'cause I practice
Every day. Every time I play, someone catches a
Loss but I am not a showoff

Jahiel Stewart

I am thankful for my health
They say your health is your wealth
Listen to these rhymes
It would be a good way to spend your time
Living the way I am
I wouldn't trade it for a dime

Jahmar Sullivan

If I could, my life would be different
It wouldn't be full of awards or medals or fame
But self-accomplishments and feeling good about myself
If I could, I would leave to a quiet place and think
Only about how different my life could be
If I could, my life would be different

If I could, I would change the world
No more crimes or suffering, but peace and love for everyone

No more racial comments, but friends and family everyone
If I could change the world

If I could be like him (Messi)
I would be right up there, with respect and glory
And awards and fame
If I could be like him.

His kicks and his glory are one of a kind
He's got drama on his head, but he's cool and calm
His trophies are a treasure and his left foot is an artifact
Oh wait! It's Messi! That's who I'm talking about!

DARELL TAVAREZ

Quotes of the Day

"Without dedication there can be no progress."

"The pessimist sees difficulty in every opportunity while the optimist sees opportunity in every difficulty."

MR. ZEIGLER
Class 807

Cassidy Agard
Shanna Ally
Harry Alphonso
Muhammad Ambrose
Lilawatie Bajnauth
Anthonie Balki
Walter Bhola
Richard Brown
Richard Davis
Arianne Deoraj
Bisma Erbab
Elvilisse Espinal
Lamar Fousheé-Rogers
Savitri Hariram
Shivanie Harkishun
Almad Hill
Aliyah Hoshing
Aquana Lewis
Dreama Pickens
Dhanwantie Ramlochan
Alicia Santos
Aneesa Sheriff
Taranbir Singh
Britney Solomon
Xavier Spencer
Shaquan Thomas

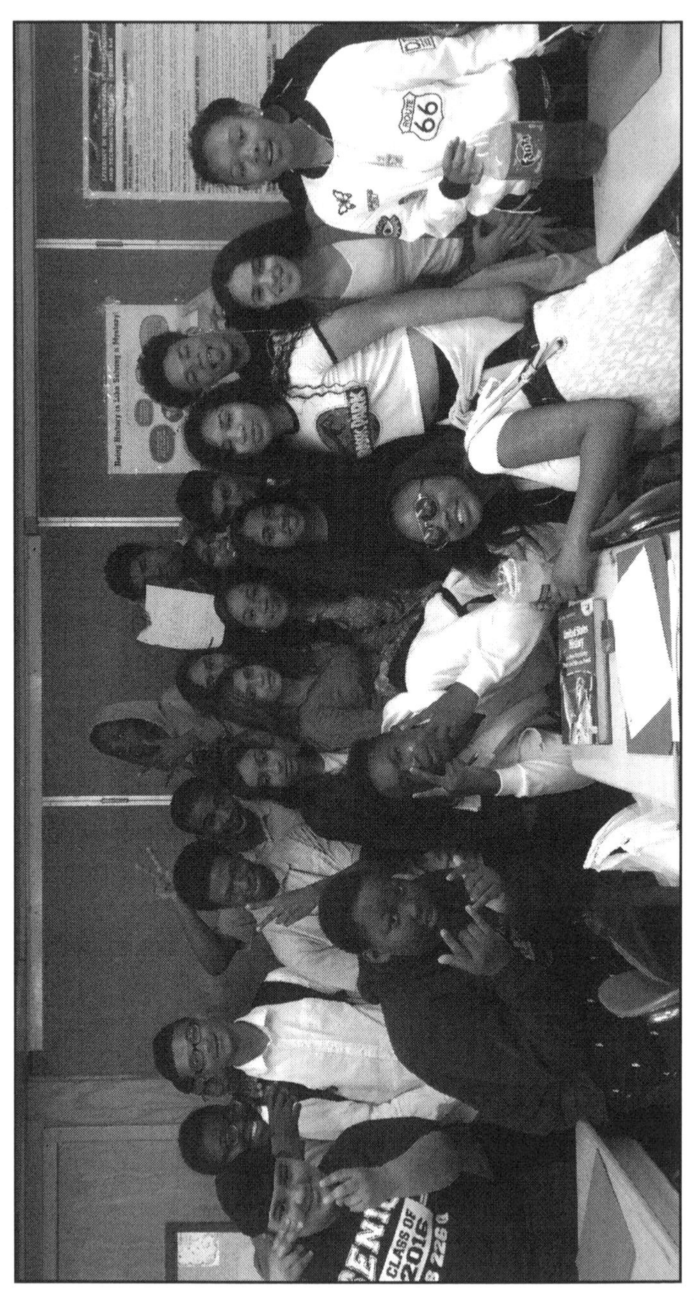

CLASS 807

From Class 807

A Class Poem is a poem that happens from a brainstorming session. Different students call out lines and we collaborate until we are satisfied.

Loyalty to
One person is
Very important
Except when you lose it

Find your way to success
Pick the choice that fits you best
But you cannot give up
Things will get rough
But always chase your goals
Don't forget
You are the one in control
Only you can decide
Which road holds the key to success
People will try to bring you down
Play you off as a clown
But you know who you are
So you must stay proud
The road to success is quite difficult
But stay focused
Don't lose hope
Your reward will be the most

CASSIDY AGARD

Where I'm from
There's no playing around
You gotta work hard just to start

Where I live
There's a beach right by me
You just look out of the window
And you'll feel the breeze

Where I'm from
Everyone is loving
But make the wrong friends
And you'll get enemies

Where I'm now everyone is loving
And caring
You don't have to worry about a single thing

Where I'm from and
Where I am now
Shares two different memories
The ones from the past and the
One from now

SHANNA ALLY

She cheated on me
And hurt my feelings
I was over here still loving her
For no reason

People say I'm dumb for
Going back
But I'm not the only dumb one
As she gave me another chance
I was on vacation
Not knowing what she was saying

I found out the hard way
That we had broken up
She lied about me
And covered up her story

I was staying loyal
Through the whole thing
But one day I broke
And confronted her
Until she gave in

Her name was Nebraska
Moving along with Alaska

HARRY ALPHONSO

Success?
How would anyone define success?
For me
I think of it as the silver spoon
On the delicious sundae
Or the absolute gold pile
That took years to dig
Through countless years

Now that being said
I think of it as a treasure
That I'll keep forever
In my hands
Filled with blisters, cuts
And all sorts of things, too

MUHAMMAD AMBROSE

I cannot see it
I cannot taste it
I cannot smell it

What is it?

I can only feel it
Such an intense feeling
A deep feeling
A wonderful falling
It makes me warm
On the inside

What is it?

It makes me feel alive
I feel as if I can
Do anything
When I get this amazing feeling

I cannot see it
I cannot taste it
I cannot smell it

What is it?
What is this feeling?

Love

LILAWATIE BAJNAUTH

The worst feeling
Is when
Someone makes you feel special
Then suddenly leaves you
Hanging
And you have to act like
You don't care at all

All the pieces of my heart
Breaks and fall
Until someone special
Comes into my life

And fixes it all

ANTHONIE BALKI

What's My Style?

I like to play games
Staying up at night late
Going to the part to play
Sports without breaks

WALTER BHOLA

I only have one friend
In my life

We talk every day and night
We share our money
Without owing it back

Because I know we always
Got each other's back
Since 6th grade
We were young playing with
Thumb tacks

Playing video games
While people were
Outside selling crack

Only we were in it together
We even might be
Friends forever

We celebrate each other's birthday
Every single year
He is my best friend
No longer my peer

We've been friends for 5 years
Now that deserves a cheer!

RICHARD BROWN

Take a Stand
Lend a Hand
Stop Bullying!

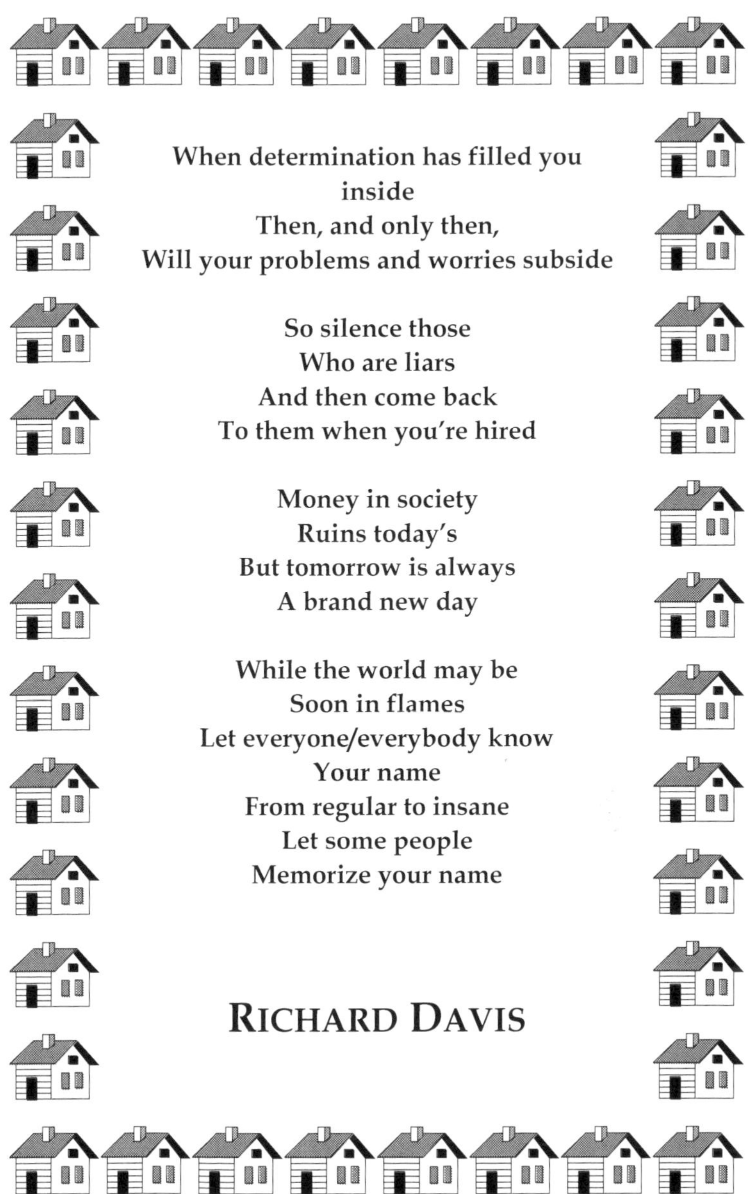

When determination has filled you
inside
Then, and only then,
Will your problems and worries subside

So silence those
Who are liars
And then come back
To them when you're hired

Money in society
Ruins today's
But tomorrow is always
A brand new day

While the world may be
Soon in flames
Let everyone/everybody know
Your name
From regular to insane
Let some people
Memorize your name

RICHARD DAVIS

Sometimes I wonder
Why I am here
And how I was in the
Early years

Sometimes I wonder why
Is there so much hate
But from the government's mistakes
The African Americans they hung are late

Sometimes I think of why I exist
Is it to balance out the drama
Through my family and future kids?

Sometimes
Almost always
I ask why do we exist
It is a long tale from the truth
And we still don't get the gist

RICHARD DAVIS

When I grow up
A criminal psychologist
Is what I'll be

The doctors will come to me
They'll show me respect
Hopefully on them
I will reflect

From me criminals will learn
Maybe they will turn

They will become good
As I know they could

I'll cure them all
And be sure to catch them
When they fall

ARIANNE DEORAJ

My best friend and I
go through thick and thin
She is my bestie, my other half
and forever my best friend

She's the reason
I don't give up when I feel
Like giving up

She will be the first to help
I love her and forever have
This lovely girl
By my side

Alexsis will be
The only person going
Through the ups and downs
With me

Bisma Erbab

When I grow up
I want to fight crime
Just put my mind to it
Like Criminal Minds

It's not easy to find the bad guys
But you always got to try
And when you find them
There's no sense in
Asking them why

Elvilisse Espinal

When I am successful
I'll be the master of art
It won't just be a hobby
I'm gonna take it to heart

Gonna be making mad money
While doing what I love
I'm using this gift
That God sent me from above

This talent is going to make
The whole world smile
As far as I know
I won't retire for a while

Lamar Fousheé-Rogers

Life is a game
A challenge for everyone
Everyone needs to play
It's not really all that fun

There are challenges
That everyone goes through
But not all pass their level
Something holds them back
And maybe
Gets them in trouble

There is one challenge
That most people find hard
And that is love
Most people take their lovers
To see the stars
Others make them forget
Who they are

Life is testing everyone
You don't have a choice
If you want to play
You can ask for help
But you need to go your own way

Savitri Hariram

This is for you
The one that makes me drool
My life is incomplete
Without you

You are my heart and soul
You and I both know
This is true
I love you, Food
And you love me, too!

SAVITRIE HARIRAM

Best friend, best friend
Oh where do you be?

I miss you so much
It's like you left me

Best friend, best friend
I love you so much
I can't imagine
What life would be without you

Best friend, Best Friend
Please come back
I miss you and I love you
To the moon and back

SHIVANIE HARKISHUN

Grandma said . . .

Grandma said
Watch who are your friends
They're just here
To play pretend

When you're left
And have no life
Friends will be quick
To get out of sight

All they want is stack
How much you wanna bet
They ain't gonna never
Have your back

Grandma said
Having friends may seem whack
But just that
Will keep you on track

ALIYAH HOSHING

My Ode goes to my girlfriend
For being there throughout
The day
I'm so happy that you're my bae

Even when I sometimes frown
You're always there to make me smile

You're the second queen
On the throne
You are my spine
The most important bone

You're my everything
You'll never be replaced
Feels like I won a trophy
Feels like I won "First Place"!

ALMAD HILL

I've seen my goal since the 2nd grade
That's why I fear no soul
They can't bring me down

I'm not gonna turn out like these
Fools on the street
I'm gonna have beautiful jewelry
And great shoes on my feet

I hang around people that have goals like me
And believe in my dreams

When I am successful
I'll be in Greece
So I can see everyone
At my meet & greets

I'll be in my private jet and
You'll see me dressing at my best

I'll take my mother shopping
When she leaves
She'll be looking popping

Aquana Lewis

When life is holding me down
I have to always remember
I'm striving for the crown
"Nobody can ever bring me down
Because when y'all fooling around
I won't be around

When the hate don't work
They start telling lies
That's why I
Stay on my grind
So I wont rewind

People always doubt me
But yet know nothing about me

DREAMA PICKENS

Love is when someone loves

Only you and just for who you are

Valentine's Day is to show more love

Even if you are mad, just continue loving the person that's always, always there for you

DHANWANTIE RAMLOCHAN

Success is my inspiration, my motivation
My determination
But the clock is ticking
And my time is wasting
My problems are rising
And I'm drowning
But I won't let it
Get in my way
I will climb the highest mountain
And tame the untamable
To get where I'm headed
Because I am a survivor
And I... will survive
I can already see me
Caring for the kids
Putting a smile on their faces and
Living my dreams
Loving to help the most in need
And when you look at me
You'll see I have the
Job of my dreams!

ALICIA SANTOS

Success isn't something
That can be bought
Just give me a chance
I just need one shot
Sure, they'll doubt me at first
But soon they'll see
I'm not the worst

Believe if you
want
That I've got no
game
But in the end
I'll have all of the
fame

When I grow up
I want to be a musician
Playing through the day
Feeling like I'm winning

Although I've got a long while to go
I'll show everyone
That I'm a pro!

Aneesa Sheriff

What's My Style?

I like to travel the world
And meet lots of girls
Girls I can dance with
And even give pearls

What's My Style?

I like to play games
Which sometimes takes days
Because I play games that are crazed
But give me a whole lot of fame

What's My Style?

I like to wake up late
And go on a lot of dates
Then I eat a lot of cake
Which I appreciate

You can ask my friend Bill Gates
He knows I'm not a fake
He also knows I went on a date
With his wife
It was fate.

TARANBIR SINGH

Sometimes I wonder
Why they don't believe
Sometimes I wonder
When they could stop
They make me feel
I don't belong on the earth
But I'll make it with all my worth

Sometimes I wonder
How to go on
Sometimes I wonder
Should I be gone?
Should I run away or stay here

Sometimes I wonder
Why they do this to me
Sometimes I think it's just cruelty
Maybe it's the actions ...
No it's just the words

Words hurt more than actions
By maybe it's my re-action

BRITNEY SOLOMON

Around the way
Riding bikes, playing sports
Only one not stopping short
Understanding my path way
Not leaving without a mark on the world
Drawing my life inside of a pearl

This is it
The time is near
Hear the breaks
Engine stopping with no fear

Wait for it
A new beginning
Yes, I'm dreaming the future of a new ending

XAVIER SPENCER

Best friends are alright
I mean okay
But make a wrong turn
And they'll go insane

They lie, they cheat
They think you don't matter
When you try to make sense
All they hear is loud chatter

They don't care what you say
They try and get their way

I swear they're the worst
I could just burst
Into laughter I mean
It's funny how they target me

I'd ignore them
I mean completely
They'll be mad when
I replace them swiftly

XAVIER SPENCER

Sometimes I wonder if
I'll make it to the NFL

Sometimes I wonder
If I could stop taking these L's

Sometimes I try my
best
To be better than
the rest

SHAQUAN THOMAS

MR. ZEIGLER
Class 808

Lincoln Adams
Chelsea Akintunde
Anjelina Alexander
Gurdyal Bisnauth
Alisha Britton
Allayah Brown
Annifa Ghanie
Amy Gomez
Renée Horne
David John
Malik Lockett
Xiare McKenzie
Kareena Naidoo
Laquidra Pearsall
Tamia Pearson
Aaron Plass
Masood Rahaman
Robert Reynoso
Pream Singh
Nyeisha Telfer
Marston Trotz

I want to be a superhero
What superhero?
I want to be Superman
You know why?
'Cuz I want to be Man of Steal
Fly, shoot laser out of my eyes
Save people
Go to outer space
With no suit
That's what I want to be

LINCOLN ADAMS

When I look into the future
I see me counting a
Stack of money
So people won't be able
To say "Ha-ha, you funny"

Being successful starts with me
It's just who I want to be

People could talk the talk
And ten come up
With an angry walk
But I got my eyes on the prize
'cuz we all know time flies

CHELSEA AKINTUNDE

"Every accomplishment begins with you."

You think you know me
But really do you know you?
You worry about what I do
You think you know me
But you only know
The outside
Take a second and dig deeper
What's on the inside of me
Is broken into pieces
But I stay strong
For myself and family
Don't be quick to judge someone
Because you don't know what's
On the inside

Anjelina Alexander

Friendship is like sugar
When mixing it in hot water
It dies
Mix it in cold water
It sticks around for a while
Hot water is like lying
Hot water is betrayal
Cold water is like loyalty
Cold water is like trust
Honestly, if you were a true friend
You would have told me the truth

"We are all born impregnated with greatness but don't show it."

A friend is someone we turn to
When our spirits need a lift

A friend is someone we treasure
For our friendship is a gift

A friend is someone who fills our lives
With beauty, joy and grace
And makes the world we live in
A better and happier place

GURDYAL BISNAUTH

My success is my dream
If I don't try
Then it will always be a dream
When I succeed
Everyone will love me
But I'm going to say move away from me
I'm not a game
So I will not be played
But if you try to play me
You will be slayed
But when I succeed
If you need me I will help you

When I grow up
I'm gonna be rollin' up in a Benz
With the top down saying "what's up?"
Then everyone that doubted me is gonna say
Lisha got rich and really did it her way

When I look into the future
This is what I'll do
Get in my Benz and cruise
Down the street and count my tens
Then I'ma be sayin' "Peace"

When I look in the mirror
I see a pediatrician
Helping cure all the babies
Of malnutrition

Like a soldier on a mission
My babies are healthy, wealthy and rich
And it ain't gonna switch!

Alisha Britton

Starts with no one but me
I have to see and believe
That life can be hard
But I can achieve and receive
Anything that comes my way
And trust me
It won't be on delay

My mama always said
Do everything to the fullest
But really
Can I do this?

My excuse is always
I don't have time
But I have to do what I have to do
And that's the bottom line
At the end of the day
I have to choose
What I have to do

Allayah Brown

My style is colorful
And fun
And when I'm done
I'ma look like I won

My style is also laid back
And cool
And when I dance
Count 1, 2 3 and I'll move

I like my hair low and slayed
When I walk past people
It looks like I'm about to get paid

What's my style?
I like playing ball

ALLAYAH BROWN

When you want to smile
But you have to cry
When you are feeling fine
But your goals have died

Don't give up
And don't you quit
Smile, stand tall
And make sure it's not a dream

Make sure it's happening
And make sure no one stops you

Make sure you don't give up and
Don't You Quit

ANNIFA GHANIE

"Stop violence, Drop money and Roll the dice"

A best friend is someone
You can count on
Someone who
You can lean on
But me ...

I used to have one
But it didn't end well
It made my heart broken
Making me think we were like sisters
It hurt so much I almost fell ...

Now. Right now
I won't be the same
But I hope soon I'll be ok

I feel like a broken plate
I feel like a ripped up piece of paper
One day there will be glue
And one day
There will be tape

I will be waiting ...

ANNIFA GHANIE

I once had a best friend
One that I took everywhere with me
Wherever the place may be

I remember the day
I bought him for a dollar
I thought he'd still be with me
When I'm older
And got taller

But then I lost him
And I almost cried
I could of died

I lost him out in the rain
I was in pain

"Dedicated to Pickles."

AMY GOMEZ

Sometimes life can
Seem a little uneasy
But you can make it
Better for you by going to others
To see what they do

To move along from all sorrows
To happiness
Just to make your life as easy as
You want it to be

When I look into the future
I'll look like this
A woman stacking her cash
Like a ball going swish!

I'll be calling the shots
While I'm reaching for the top
Riding in my drop top

When I look into my future
I'll look like this
A business woman
Keeping everything classy and clean

When I look into the future
I'll be better than I am now
Won't be perfect
But still successful

RENÉE HORNE

Friendship is
Commitment
Love and Trust

The awesome power of Loyalty
Honesty is a must

When I'm on my
Last two feet
Will true friends
Be there for me

I need friends
That are strong and sweet
To just lend a hand

DAVID JOHN

Success, you accomplished everything
You needed to
And you will be able
To have money, too!

After that
You can do whatever you want to do
I know I'm rhyming
That's because I have good timing

I don't know what to say
So should I pray
Or should I just stop my poem
And go away. . . Hmmm
I know this doesn't have
Anything to do with success
But I'm sure when I grow up
I'll be the best
I'll have children, a wife
And a J.O.B.
And watch
Nobody's gonna be able to
Stop me ...

MALIK LOCKETT

Music is
A beat of a song where
You feel lost and
You feel drugged up
Somewhere that you
Can escape from this world

A way to free yourself
From the darkness
And try to find a way
Out of it

Finally you
think to yourself
These lyrics of a song that
Touches your soul and
That understands you

XIARE MCKENZIE

When I grow up I want to be a doctor
And help people feel
Better than they did
When they asked what's the deal

I'll be like
I don't know
How to feel
Is this real?

Am I really accomplishing my dream?

Kareena Naidoo

One day I am going to become a vampire
I am going to fly higher
In the sky
And wave bye-bye
You will see me no more
Because I will be on a tour
With my other vampire friends
That are hard core

I will be biting human beings
Ingesting their inner feelings
Living long
And feeling strong

Laquidra Pearsall

Yes! I am dark skin, thick and
Have short hair
But I am confident in my skin
People rate me as a 3 and a 4
But I am a high 10
You know what—forget about it
Don't put numbers on me
My name is Laquidra
But you can call me LAQLUI
That stands for Lovely, Athletic, Quite Loud
Unique and Independent
And yeah, that's just me!

When I grow up
I'm gonna be a hairstylist
A hairstylist because I
Like doing hair

I like doing hair because
I'm good at it
Great at it
'Cause I been doing it since I was young
'Cause since I was young I had doll babies
Doll babies because I
Liked how they look
Liked how they look because
They had hair
And fake earrings

TAMIA PEARSON

What's my style?
My style is the best
It's about working in a doctor's office
And doing blood tests
And telling people about
The illness they have
To make it better than the rest
On the Ave

What's my Style?

My style is being the helper
The example to the community
And the greatest leader

My style is the best
It's about being better and having success
Which is better than the rest

Aaron Plass

Food is
My most favorite thing in the world
I love all kinds of food
That makes my head twirl

Everyone knows I love food, dude
Because you already know
"Masood loves food"

I'm not a bad guy
Neither am I rude

Now let me move on from that
Tell you something
About myself
I'm not a book worm
I don't keep books on my shelf

MASOOD RAHAMAN

They don't know it
But I work hard every day
'cause later—I'm in the NBA
Pulling up like Clay

Education comes first
Can't say nothing at all
It's a drag but nothing
stopping me
From playing ball

When I grow up
I'm gonna be a leader
And get wins for my team
Playing ball that was my
dream
Before I was a teen
You know me

It's all water when
I pull up for a 3
And I ain't stopping
Until I take that *W* home with me

Robert Reynoso

Friendship is like
Salad dressing
It's up to you
To see the blessing
Before the gift of betrayal
Is near go and get
The gift of care
For someone
That you trust
Because
That's a must

PREAM SINGH

I will give you life
And make you shine bright
Just because I gave you life
Doesn't mean you'll be alright
You'll keep shining bright
Until I disappear
And you'll have to take control
And steer
Because this is your life
And you gotta' continue your grind
And finish this bumpy ride
That we call life

NYEISHA TELFER

You think you know me
Well, think again
I'm like a little butterfly
Hidden in a cocoon
It appears weak and small
But eventually grows tall
And evolves into the most
Beautiful thing of all

NYEISHA TELFER

You think you know me
But you don't
You might think I'm big and
strong
But somewhere in there
Is a little soul
A calm little person
Who smiles and
Acts like a geek

MARSTON TROTZ

Quotes of the Day

"You tell the story, and then
you live the story."

Renée McRae

"Stop everything
Drop all unnecessaries
Roll in a new direction"

MR. MARCH AND MR. ZEIGLER
Class 809

Nastazia Arnold
Chris Astudillo
Mahendra Bassoo
Tiara Bridges
Anthony Bux
Elisha Drepaul
Latchman Harry
Rawf Isa
Izia Karim
Lakia Kinred
Wilner Lincifort, Jr.
Nathan Maharaj
Breanna Mason
Tina Mohamed
Mariam Moudoujy
Jordan Munro
Zyiah Murray
Nathaniel Powell
Alix Ramlagan
Javon Rhoden
Joshua Ruffin
Manpreet Singh
Shirly Solares
Juniel Torres
Sadio Toure
Andrew Vaught
Diamond Welsh
Aneesa Yasseen

CLASS 809

From Class 809

A Class Poem is a poem that happens from a brainstorming session. Different students call out lines and we collaborate until we are satisfied.

There once was an angry man
He got hit in the head with a pan
His name was Mike
He loved his bike
He said never trust a man with a black van

There once was a man named Blart
He fell on his face in a cart
He got so mad
And kicked a horse that was sad
And now he works at Walmart

MANPREET SINGH and JORDAN MUNRO

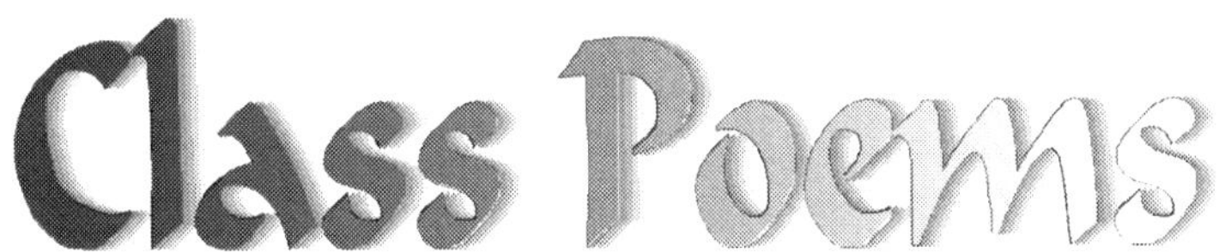

From Class 809

A Class Poem is a poem that happens from a brainstorming session. Different students call out lines and we collaborate until we are satisfied.

She lives her life alone
A girl without a phone
She has a life
She's living it right
But you know she's home alone

ANEESA YASSEEN, NASTAZIA ARNOLD, BREANNA MASON

There once was a flying fry
People knew that he never cried
His name was Bob
He had only one job
Which was to always fly in the sky

WILNER LINCIFORT, JR.

My best friend stood by me all my life
If I was a boy, I would've made her my wife
When I cried, she came and told me that I shouldn't
Because a person should be happy
And live life to the fullest
My best friend is like my diary and I am hers
We hold each other's mind and problems
Never to be told to another
When we fight, we make up in a minute
Because I would and she would cry if we had a split
We don't listen when people try to tear us apart
Cuz we both know that
We love each other from the heart
We pray that we can stay together
Cuz we love each other no matter the weather

Arnold Nastazia

When will the world stop this stupidity
Of countries hating other countries?
Explosions and killing innocent people makes no sense
It is just going to lead to world wars
And of course another world will come to an end
Before we can see our great-grandchildren
When will racism end because a person is Muslim?
You call them terrorists
And treat them as if they're inferior
Skin, hair and color doesn't matter
All humans are birds of a feather
Who are supposed to stick together
In the end, no matter what race
We are still humans with skin and hair
When will the world come together?
Or will it go down, down, down... like fire?

Great video games are really expensive at Game Stop.
Kids nowadays are interested in doing chores
In exchange for the games.
However, some kids don't even get to play them.
It's for their own good to enjoy the outdoors,
Although I like electronics
I'll look to use my savings to enjoy the latest one

"It's not what you look at that matters, it's what you see."

I looked at a clown with big shoes
And what I saw was a psycho
Respect is a powerful word
That you can earn
If you use that word,
People can respect you, too

CHRIS ASTUDILLO

Sometimes I have the power
To climb the Eiffel Tower
Sometimes I waste food
Because I'm in a bad mood
Sometimes I get really tired
Listening to this guy named Mr. Guyer
Sometimes I have the power
To take a 30 minute shower

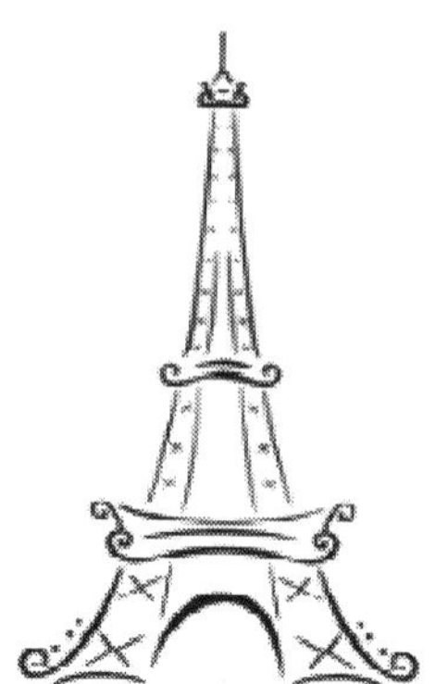

MAHENDRA BASSOO

When I think about friendship, I think about hate
Because all I know is these people are fake
The honesty is not there but hatred is
A friendship is forever
And best friends should stay together
Humor is bad without friendship

TIARA BRIDGES

I wanna succeed and I ain't got no time
I wanna get straight A's
And I wanna be successful in life
But I don't have anyone bringing me down
And I just gotta keep my head up
And keep my eyes on the crown

ANTHONY BUX

I am strong and I know right from wrong
I stay strong through the long day gone
I wake to see what's there for me
Sometimes I think, "where is he?"
Then I remember, he's there for me
He's in Heaven, my lucky number is seven
One day when we die, we'll all go to Heaven

ELISHA DREPAUL

Sometimes I wish to grow up and get a job and...
Sometimes I hate when people yell at me and...
Sometimes I like when people treat me kindly.
Sometimes I want my dreams
Sometimes I fall in love
Sometimes I feel I'm in Heaven
And I really want to come down
Sometimes I just want to die and go to Heaven

LATCHMAN HARRY

Halloween is my favorite holiday
Always has lots of fun
Likes to be with my friends
Likes to read scary stories
Orange juice tastes good to me
Wears a bird costume
Eats good food
Eats a lot of candy
Never gets enough candy

Rawf Isa

Really likes to go to the store
Am from Yemen
Works hard on my homework
Football is my favorite sport
I like food and
Swimming in the pool
Always enjoys chicken and french fries

Grandparents are the best things that can happen to you
They love you and they get you out of trouble
Grandmothers make fresh cookies or biscuits
I wish I had my grandmother
I lost her New Years 2010
I can't tell you about grandfathers
Because mine died one week before I was born

Lakia Kinred

I am a man who stands up tall and brave
When I have things to do, I go do them
I am a fighter and a winner
When I see people suffer,
I get thinner for some reason
I am determined to get things done
When I'm finished with life, I am gone

I will survive if I do good in life
In life, humans are born and humans are gone
If you work really hard you will succeed
But if you don't, life will be a bad deed

Izia Karim

Football is not a test
It's something you play to be the best
You could be the light
And you could be the shadow
But guess what...
I am that light that shines bright
And gives it everything I have

Wilner Lincifort, Jr.

"It's not what you look at that matters, it's what you see."

I looked at a Burger King employee at McDonald's
I saw him stealing Big Macs

I have regrets about everything that made you sad
I shouldn't have done them, and I know they were bad
I wish I could fix this, just for you
And then I could be your honey boo-boo
If you can't accept that, then that's fine
But I will remember that you were once mine

NATHAN MAHARAJ

Love is what warms a heart
Love is caring and sweet
Love can't be placed on a chart
Love is always unique
Love is honesty
Love is respect
Love is what makes you
Not want to regret
Love is awesome
Love is great
Love can be eaten
As breakfast, on a plate

BREANNA MASON

I don't understand life
It changed me into someone I hate
It's made me think about horrible things
And turned me into its victim

I hate it so much
Sometimes I feel like I want to escape
I feel like I could die
But I don't want to
I might say I do but I don't
I just want to be happy
But every time I become happy
The problems turn around and hit me

It's like I can't escape
I'm stuck in this place
Where no one knows how to love
People leave and never come back
I'm hurting on the inside and smiling on the out
But then there's this person that makes me so happy
But no one's perfect
And that person messes up sometimes

I can't lie—it hurts
But what is love
No matter how many definitions you get
You'll never know
Love and life are a mystery
Just waiting to unfold
But the question is:
Will you let it?

TINA MOHAMED

"It's not what you look at that matters. It's what you see."

I looked at a boy playing
And saw a future NBA player.

When you have courage
Then come to me
I need you to be truthful with me
You need to give me
Honesty
And I'll do the same
And that's what you call
RESPECT

MARIAM MOUDOUJY

Bullies are mean
They have no life
They pick on others
And think it's right
So I'll stand up
And take the fight
Because picking on others
Is just not right
Will you join me?

JORDAN MUNRO

You think that you know me
My family is going through a lot
But we solve it together no matter what
My dad gave up everything for me
For half of my life, he was always at work, see
Now, he wants the best for us
And is starting over for the rest of us
Both my parents started over with us
To help us forward our education
And become successful men, like my dad

JORDAN MUNRO

Sometimes I laugh and sometimes I cry
But sometimes I believe that I
Am not controlling my life
Sometimes I feel emotion and things come out
But isn't that what life is about?

Sometimes I make mistakes but I don't regret
Because I know I've proven a point
I think you know what I'm saying

Sometimes I'm empty alone inside
Because I'm in a new school
And I feel like I'm gonna fall
Fall so hard that I can't get back up

Just because I know a couple of people here
Doesn't mean I feel better
Maybe I should start all over
And write it down in a letter

ZYIAH MURRAY

I'm from that part of Brooklyn, that's where I live
But the future's in front of me and the past is behind
Bet you in ten years, you'll see a sophisticated woman
And wish you were me

When I look in the mirror, this is what I see
A successful singer at the VMA's

If I ran, I would spit bars like dreg
Nowadays I'm not really focused on drama
My mind is on the riches and my future
All I see is fame and fortune
But for right now I'm focused
More on money than on people
Because I never met a dollar I didn't like

NATHANIEL POWELL

Remember, I ain't had nothing
Going to school, lookin' bummy with my grades low
Now I'm rocking all the designers
Working on my grades to be higher
So I can make my family proud
Thought I forgot about my struggles?
That's a damned lie
All the people I look up to or I'm chilling with
Either dead or turned fake
These bullets got no I.D.
Either be cold-hearted or get used
I eat with the same people I starve with

ALIX RAMLAGAN

If I could I would
Stop all the pain
And be successful
And make a big change
I'd stop all the violence
Because gangs are lame
And it will always be sunny
No time for rain
I love to stunt
And I love to style
But I have to work hard
Because Heaven's right up the mile

JAVON RHODEN

Sometimes I wish
That I could have it good
I have both parents
But still live in the hood
My father dropped out of high school
And got a job and a place to live
And he tries his best
To support all of his kids
My mom is so smart
But doesn't have all the knowledge
That's why she's working
And still going to college
I'm giving you the truth,
I ain't gonna fake it
I gotta do what I gotta do
So I can make it

I have a lot of determination
I'm shootin' and runnin'
While some kids in the hood
Ain't doing nothin' but puffin'
So you see I need concentration
To work on my determination
I don't need people bringing me down
Because at the end
I'ma be the one with the crown

Sometimes I wonder
Will I become what I wanna be
Or will I become a homeless man
Sleeping on the street
All people have dreams
But some can't make them reality
Don't you see
I'm trying to be the best
At what I want to be

JOSHUA RUFFIN

Sometimes I wonder
What the world has become
A lot of people are homeless
And some think it's fun
I want to give back
But don't know what to do
Maybe I can give
Somebody some food
But in the end
I want to have fun
Probably play a game
Or get my homework done
It's hard to balance
Both pain and fun

Manpreet Singh

When will we stop this violence
That is making our country worse and worse.
When will we have a big reunion
And talk about what could happen
And what we can do to make the world better?
A lot of people think that violence is good.
Well, let me tell you something,
It's not good.

Shirly Solares

I see you every day
When I see you
I think about you

You feel like we're friends
I feel like we're more than friends
If you said no, it's okay
But I will never give up
I might try without success
But I won't be a mess
I'll be okay and move on today
So I'll focus on my career and pay

Juniel Torres

Sometimes I wonder why should I strive
Success is important but why should I cry
This is my life, so don't even try
Your life is important, just like mine

Sometimes I wonder if this is a crime
Guns everywhere, making people die
Sometimes I wonder if I can survive
With this world so full of crime
Extinction is coming soon why should I
This world is full of nothing except dies and cries

Sadio Toure

Life is like a piece of gum on the ground
People walk by and step on it
Until they pick it up off the bottom of their shoe
You have one chance at it
So don't let it overwhelm you 'til you take your own

ANDREW VAUGHT

You can look at someone and think they've got it good
That's because you're blinded by the jewelry
Their looks change the way you see them
Make-up, jewelry
Hides the brokenness and sadness inside
Know someone
Before blinding yourself with their beauty

DIAMOND WELSH

Friendship is not about the years of being known
It's about loyalty, trust and sacrifice that you can show
People fight, families fight and friends, too
But making up is the commitment
Commitment is not just talking regularly
My meaning of commitment is someone who is there
Through thick and thin, high and low, loud and quiet
And shallow but deep

DIAMOND WELSH

This bond between us
Is strong and unbreakable
No one, not even you and I,
Are able to break it
You shine the light on me
When I see darkness coming
I drown but you always bring me
Back from the depths of my mind
Our unconditional love
Is beyond compare

ANEESA YASSEEN

When will the time come
Where I can really live?
When can I see the world
And all it's hidden beauty?

Quotes of the Day

"Do not forsake wisdom, and she will protect you. Love her, and she will watch over you."

"Many are called but few get up."

MR. MARCH AND MS. SANGHAVI
Class 810

Saffiya Amirulla
Dhaneshwar Attloo
Xavier Baez
Nicolas Blair
Tyra Caleb
Sean Chan
Imani Chung
Candacey Dutchin
Anupa Gulab
Javon Byrd
Wendell Guthrie
Bibi Hawaldar
Shiphrah Holland
Aliyah Hoshing
Zameena Hussain
Neilajah Hyman-Charles
Geovany Ixco
Luke Murray
Jashveer Pahalad
Caleb Paillant
Arelle Palmer
Eugene Pearson
Karran Persaud
Jason Pullay
Rachel Ramdeo
Quindell Rice
Zianna Smith
Anadalay Tamayo
Anastazia Tyz
Kelvin Yorrick

CLASS 810

Dear Ms. Renée ... by Class 810

"First of all, I love Ms. Renée. If you ask me why, well it's because she inspired me about my future, my life, and I had the most wonderful time with her. She is a person who has great talent, respect and understanding." Candacey Dutchin

"This program with Ms. Renée was fun. I wrote my thoughts and expressed how I feel. It helped me not be as shy. For example, I was too shy to play basketball in this school, and now I play a lot and I'm getting better at it." Caleb Paillant

"I enjoyed this program because it helped me to see who I really am. It helped me get a better grade in ELA class, and it allowed me to see my true talents. I love Miss Renée. She is the best!" Saffiya Amirulla

"Ms. Renée was and still is an amazing teacher. She does her job so well, and her poems and rhymes are so on point. She should be a regular teacher at this school." Anupa Gulab

"I don't write poetry or raps, but when she made me do it, I started to like it. It was like putting everything I want to do successfully in life into a poem or rap." Arelle Palmer

"She really showed me more about what I wanted to do when I get older. Also she taught me not to be afraid and to keep on pushing to get to where I would like to be life. I thank Ms. Renée for that." Neilajah Hyman-Charles

"Her class was the best. She's fun and cool. Also I wish she stayed ... now class won't be the same." Jason Pullay

"The Step/Write into Your Greatness program with Ms. Renée helped me to realize that if you're not scared or if you overcome your fear, you can do anything." Shiphrah Holland

"This program was a very unique program in my opinion and experience. I think that this program was just as awesome as science. I personally liked it because it helped me to create poems which I never thought I could have created." Karran Persaud

"When I first saw Ms. McRae I knew she was a powerful woman. From the way I see things, you knew what you came here for was to teach us how to believe in ourselves." Zianna Smith

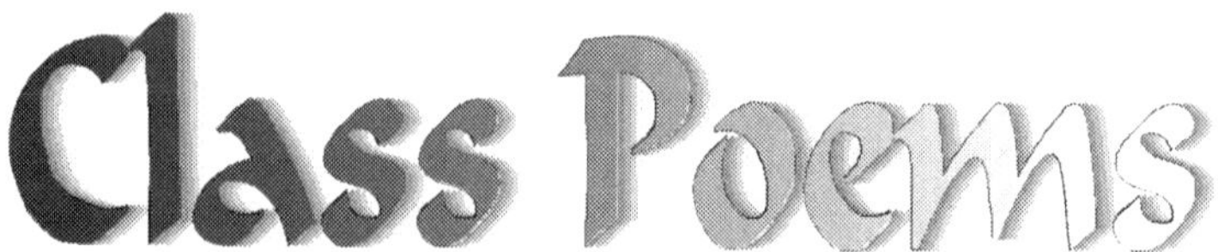

From Class 810

A Class Poem is a poem that happens from a brainstorming session. Different students call out lines and we collaborate until we are satisfied.

Life is a privilege
You know this is divine
If you don't live your life
You're wasting your time

Learn to live
Your life to the fullest
Don't look back
Even if you're clueless

I love my mother above all things
I love the way she talks and sings
She treats me like her special rose
She dries my tears and sadness goes
She is gentle, patient, meek and kind
The nicest mother you can find
Every night I pray
"God bless My mother
Because she's the best!"

SAFFIYA AMIRULLA

When I look into the mirror,
I see a dynamic figure
When I look into the water
I see my true color
When I look into the sky
I see my smile
When I look into my heart
I see why I smile

When I grow up, I want to fly
And see the how and see the why
I want to paint flowers of blue
And see their shape coming true

When I see my future day by day
I see my picture going my way

Love Love Love

Love is your life
You know love is your future
Love can make you live
Love can make you die
Love can make you get married
Love can make you cry

Dhaneshwar Attloo

I love playing basketball
I would be disappointed in myself
If I gave up
I want to stay focused
But before I accomplish my goals
I need a rhythmic flow
Shooting threes is my passion
I shoot with such fashion
I like driving to the basket
When I make the shot
They will blow a gasket

Xavier Baez

I am thankful
For my family
My classmates
My friends
I am thankful
For my school
My godparents
My teachers
I am thankful
That I can play basketball
So I can achieve my goals
I am thankful that
I am intelligent

Nicolas Blair

I am Fall
With the beautiful colors on the trees
I am Fall
Subtle and nice, just as I was born to be
I am Fall
I have good days and bad days
But always keep a smile on my face
I am Fall
Not everyone's favorite
I am Fall
When everything is over
I break off one by one
Fighting to keep it together but can't
I am Fall

Tyra Caleb

Imagine all your fears
And all your dreams
Came true
Would you be happy
Or would you be blue
Some people dream
Everyone does
But when dreams come true
You all run crying boo hoo
Fear is pain
And pain is fear
Fish fear the pain
From the living spear
Is fear real
Or pretending to be king
Like a spider
On a webbed swing

TYRA CALEB

Love is more than kissing and cuddling
It's about pushing each other to do better
Love is believing you two can grow together
Have fun times while holding hands
In the summer air
Love that hurts
Is not really love
Sometimes holding on
Hurts more
Than letting go

TYRA CALEB

I am a holiday
Nice and colorful
So much snow
Too much to shovel
In the morning
We sit at the tree
And open big surprising goodies
After that we all have fun
Too much mess to clean
But after that we all have fun
Playing games and living life

Sean Chan

Love ain't never been so hard
Stop fussin' and let me get up in your heart
You don't even know what you're missing
I could be cooking for you in your kitchen

Imani Chung

Sometimes I remember wonder dream forget want feel wish
I'll let my soul smile through my eyes
I may gather rich smiles in my heart
I admire the sunset and beauty of the moon
I put my soul and heart into my mind
I said to my soul, be still and wait for hope
As for my soul, it can't find a staircase to Heaven
Unless it be through Earth's loveliness

Candacey Dutchin

"It's not what you look at; it's what you see."

I looked at terrorists attacking Paris
And I saw some lonely, desperate people

You walk past her every day
You stop her heart in every way
You look in her direction
And you give her head confusion
You make her smile, you make her blush
Stay in her life
Because you make her day

I am quiet on the outside
But wild on the inside
When I'm in my corner
My mind is never in order
They say I never speak
But to me that's unique
I'll never change for you
If you don't like me
Sorry boo

ANUPA GULAB

I am positive and strong
I am worth
I am willing to do more
I am a helper
My life is a car that doesn't stop
I am a confident person
I never give up
I have a dream
I make it my life
You must achieve your dream
And never let it go
Life is a dream
Just waiting to be real

JAVON BYRD

Motivation keeps the body flowing
You might get old
And probably stop going
Never stop ... sweat still dripping
One day the strong will die
The weak will never lie
Life is like a slice of pie
Give the weak strength
To move on forward
Steps rise
Building still under construction

WENDELL GUTHRIE

I'll be dreaming of me
While I'm sipping my tea
I don't care about success
I want money
Not the fame
People take the easy way out
And play little games
While others on tv
Show fame or shame
I'll be in my zone
With a whole lot of money
It's funny how
The summer really changed me
I want to be in my thirties
With five daughters
And ten cars
Since last year,
It stopped being about me
I turned the tables
In the industry
Meanwhile everyone's thinking
About the next president
I don't care
I want to be
A high end citizen

Wendell Guthrie

"It's not what you look at; it's what you see."

I look at her
She was rude to her friends
What I saw was that she had parents
That had no respect.

Bibi Hawaldar

SOMETIMES I REMEMBER
How my heart was broken
When my parents told me
I had to migrate to another country
I missed my freedom
And I missed my friends
I remember my school
I remember my friends

Happiness is important
You know it as joy
If you don't have happiness
You're a kid without a toy.

BIBI HAWALDAR

I am your goal
I am the future you
I am the reason you did well in school
80s and 90s just to make it to me
Don't give up now
I really want us to meet
Our future together
Is only success
Honor roll and 90s
Come on, you did your best
Depression and sadness
Is just a made-up thing
Remember, I am your goal
So keep pushing
And see what your future brings

SHIPHRAH HOLLAND

"It's not what you look at; it's what you see."

I looked at kids fighting
I saw them just playing

You have to be committed
You have to be courageous
You have to think like a pro
And be a little loving too
You have to love the sport
Or anything you do
You have to be confident
Just pour your heart into it
If you want to be successful
These steps will get you moving

SHIPHRAH HOLLAND

I am...
A dinosaur
The one who runs around and roars
Sharp teeth and claws
All there but do no harm

I am...
Grandpa's princess
The one who said I would
Do better than the rest
I am Grandpa's warrior
Even when I am down
I stand tall

I am...
The girl in the hood
I wish one day to run away
And play in the woods
The tears I cried forever I hide
Even when I break down
You can't keep me down
Because I'll switch my frown
And walk around with a crown

I am...
A baller
On the court I feel taller
Even if I'm a little smaller
Shooting around
Making threes, I'm Curry
Everyone else sees me
Moving in a hurry
Threes in three seconds
I ain't never gonna rest
Until I become the best

ALIYAH HOSHING

I am the girl who doesn't care
About what people have to say about me
I am who I am
I believe in myself
I believe I can do it
I am the one who is
Likely to make people smile
Those who know me better
Know I will be there for them
I am who I am
No one can change me

ZAMEENA HUSSAIN

"Good friends are like stars. You don't always see them
But you always know they're there."
Christy Evans

Life is like a tree
You're born as a seed
With food and nourishment
You grow strong and tall
Through many seasons
You weather the storms
Until you're called home
And then you face the dawn

NEILAJAH HYMAN-CHARLES

I hear the music
I hear the beat
It makes me get up
On my feet
It makes me glad
And not so sad
It makes my day
Seem not so bad

GEOVANY IXCO

Love is strange in many ways
Love can change throughout the days

Family is good
Family is stressful
But family is there
When you aren't successful

GEOVANY IXCO

Family comes before friends
Family will be with you until the end
Stick with the people you know and love
They will be with you when times are tough
I love my mom and also my dad
They're the best friends I've ever had
I love my family with all my heart
If you don't feel the same
You're not that smart

LUKE MURRAY

When I look into the future
I'm in the MMA
I'm punching and kicking
Just to get my way
I'm not going anywhere
I'm here to stay
If you wish to try and beat me
You'd better get on your knees and pray

JASHVEER PAHALAD

I've got you cornered
I've got you scared
I've got you alone

You should be prepared
I have a fiery flame
And a cold staring glare
I can see in your soul
That you're not really scared
Listen kid, you're dead now
You can't run or scream or yelp
Now it's useless to call for help
I've got you right where I want you

To steal your soul
Drag you down
And watch you burn
Your one true love
Will never return

JASHVEER PAHALAD

I am thankful for light
It makes all our days so bright
I'm thankful for Martin Luther King
For my freedom he had to fight
I am thankful for my family
Because they always stay with me
Mostly my parents, my mom and dad
Even though they send me to my room
Whenever they get mad
Last but not least
I'm thankful for toilet paper
If it was not here
We'd have to wipe out tooshes with leaves
What I'm thankful for I hope never leaves

Caleb Paillant

My name is Arelle
I want to be a chef
The only reason why is because
It's my best

They say I can't cook
It tastes bad
But all I do is laugh
Because all I'm hearing is trash
I want to be on national TV
Them talking about my food
Watch it be so popular
It will be on the news

Arelle Palmer

A goal is something I hope to achieve
That is the reason I continue to breathe
Because I know when I achieve this goal of mine
I will be big time
And I know the greatest of the greatest moments
Will be mine

Eugene Pearson

I wrote your name in my song
But the world didn't like that song
I wrote your name in the sky
But the world blew it away
I wrote your name in the ocean
But the waves washed it away
I wrote your name in my heart
Now forever it will stay

Karran Persaud

I'm not going to stop fighting
To pass my classes
The funny thing is
Some people stop
Some will cheer
Some will criticize
It only matters if I believe
Stepping in to attack
Pain and bruises won't matter
As long as I come home
As a champ

Jason Pullay

Family is always there for you
They have your back through thick and thin
Even though you'll have your ups and down
They'll always help you win

Family is everything. They are kind

And caring

My family helps me be

Intelligent and

Loyal. Therefore,

You see why family is everything to me.

When I am successful
I'll be solving everyone's cases
When you see me
I'll be going places
I'll be in everybody's faces
Protecting them from wrong
I'll be out there
And no one will question if I'm wrong

Rachel Ramdeo

Football is a skill to show how good you are

Overall it tells you when you have to work hard

Overcome that dream to grind

Tough is the key to success

Believe in yourself

Accept the dream

Love it

Live it

QUINDELL RICE

I am the person
Who expresses her feelings
Even when nobody's willing
As long as I'm living
I am the mind that
Thinks what it hears
Even though it connects
With my fears
It doesn't bother me
Because know
That I'm here

ZIANNA SMITH

Realistic friend

Only the best dog

She is smart and shy

Even when I am not there, she always waits for me
To give her a hug
You were a kind and emotional dog.
I miss you.

ANADALAY TAMAYO

Death is something that comes with life
No matter how hard you try
You just can't hide
It's not an option
Just something that comes with a gift
Death is a place where Satan stands
He lets you think you're winning
But we all know
He has the upper hand

ANASTAZIA TYZ

When I look into my future
I see myself becoming a vet
Running around the building
Helping people's pets
When I look into the mirror
I see myself turning left and right
Helping every animal in my sight
I keep all animals happy and free
Keeping away diseases ticks and fleas

ANASTAZIA TYZ

When I grow up
I wanna be like Curry
Making 30 out of 30 in the first quarter
Shooting like I'm the best
MJ and the rest
Dunking on everybody
Like D Rose back then
When he was the best
Let me step cuz I can't tell you the rest
Just come to my games
And watch me do my best

KELVIN YORRICK

Quotes of the Day

"Success doesn't happen to you

It happens through you"

Renée McRae

If you think you can, you will.

If you think you can't, you won't.

Either way, you're right.

Ralph Waldo Emerson

Made in the USA
Middletown, DE
10 June 2016